The Toxic Lover I Was

and My Road to Recovery

JAMES D. FERGUSON

Self Made Enterprise LLC
ISBN: 979-8-9866941-3-9
Printed in the United States of America

To the women I hurt.
I see you now. I am sorry.
I am doing the work.

contents

The Toxic Lover I Was
and My Road to Recovery

acknowledgments

To my therapist, thank you for not letting me off the hook and for never making me feel like I was beyond repair. Both things were necessary.

To the men in my life who were honest enough to challenge me and patient enough to stay while I figured things out, I am grateful beyond what words can hold.

To my faith community, thank you for teaching me that accountability and grace are not opposites.

And to the women who loved me before I knew how to receive it properly, I carry your names with humility. You were not the problem. You never were.

preface

This book was supposed to be about someone who hurt me.

I spent weeks writing it that way, casting myself as the wounded one, the man who loved too much and was taken advantage of. And parts of that were true. But the longer I wrote, the more another truth kept surfacing. One I had spent years running from.

I was also the problem.

Not in every relationship. Not in every moment. But in pattern after pattern, with woman after woman, I showed up in ways that caused real damage. I controlled. I withheld. I lied. I disappeared emotionally while staying physically present. I repeated cycles I had never bothered to examine because examining them would have required me to stop seeing myself as the victim.

This book is my attempt to stop running from that truth and start walking toward it. It is not a book about self-destruction. I still believe in grace and recovery and the possibility of becoming someone new. But grace without accountability is just a comfortable story we tell ourselves. So before I could write honestly about healing, I had to write honestly about the harm.

This is that book.

— James D. Ferguson

1

the mirror i refused to look in

For most of my adult life, I was very good at telling the story of my relationships in a way that centered my pain. She was distant. She did not appreciate me. She did not understand what I needed. I loved her, and it was not enough. That was the version I carried around, polished and practiced, ready to share at any moment with anyone willing to listen.

What I left out of that story, every single time, was my part. I left out the ways I manipulated situations to keep women off balance. The way I could sense exactly what someone needed emotionally and either withhold it strategically or offer it just enough to keep them invested. I was not doing this consciously at the time. But looking back with honest eyes, the pattern is undeniable.

* * *

I remember a woman I dated in my late twenties. She was kind, patient, and genuinely in love with me. And I spent two years running hot and cold on her. Present one week, emotionally absent the next. Telling her she was overreacting when she named what she was experiencing. Making her feel like her needs were too much. She was not too much. I was too unavailable. Those are very different things, and I confused them for years.

The mirror I refused to look in would have shown me that. But I was not ready to see what was in it. So I kept telling a different story until the story stopped being enough.

* * *

The moment the story stopped being enough came quietly, as those moments often do. I was sitting in my car outside a grocery store. I had just gotten off the phone with someone I was supposed to be in a committed relationship with, and I had just lied to her about where I had been. It was a small lie. It barely registered. And that was the problem.

The ease of it. The way I hung up the phone, and felt almost nothing. No guilt, no discomfort, just the practiced smoothness of someone who had been bending the truth for so long it had become reflex. I sat there for a long time. I did not go into the store. I just sat with the quiet that comes when you are done pretending, at least for a moment, that you are someone other than who you are.

That was the beginning. Not a dramatic breakdown. Not a confrontation or an ultimatum. Just a man alone in a parking lot, finally too tired to keep telling himself the comfortable version.

control dressed up as love

I want to talk about control because I think it is one of the most misunderstood forms of toxicity. People imagine control as domineering and obvious. Loud. Aggressive. That was not how it showed up in me. Mine was subtle. It looked like concern. It looked like caring deeply about how things went. It looked like wanting to be involved in decisions, wanting to know where she was, wanting things done a particular way. I framed all of it as love. Some of it I genuinely believed was love. It was not love. It was fear wearing love's clothing.

* * *

When you have grown up in an environment where things felt unpredictable or unsafe, control becomes a survival strategy. If I can manage the variables, I can prevent the pain. The problem is that the variables in an adult relationship are other human beings, and you cannot manage people without diminishing them.

I diminished women I cared about by making them smaller so I could feel safer. I questioned their choices in ways that eroded their confidence. I made myself the authority on what was reasonable in situations where I had no right to that authority. And when they pushed back, I did not hear it as a healthy boundary being set. I heard it as a threat to the order I depended on. So I pushed back harder, or I withdrew, which was its own form of punishment.

Understanding this did not come easy. It came slowly, through therapy, through reading, through the painful process of watching my own behavior on replay and finally calling it what it was.

* * *

There was a particular incident I have thought about many times since. I was with a woman I cared about deeply, and she told me she had made plans to spend the weekend with friends without asking me first. I did not yell. I did not make demands. I simply went quiet.

I gave her silence. The kind that fills a room and says everything without saying anything. I did not tell her she was wrong. I just let her feel the weight of my disapproval until she reconsidered. She stayed home that weekend. And I told myself she had chosen me. What I did not admit was that I had made the alternative feel costly enough that she had no real choice at all. That is not love. That is leverage. It took me years to understand the difference, and a few more years after that to stop doing it.

Healthy love does not require the other person to shrink. It does not depend on managing their access to the world so that you remain their most important variable. When I finally understood that, I also understood how much damage I had done by conflating the two.

emotionally absent, physically present

There is a particular kind of loneliness that comes from being in a relationship with someone who is there but not really there. I know this because women I loved tried to tell me that is what it felt like to be with me, and I did not believe them.

I thought because I showed up, because I was not out in the streets, because I provided and was physically faithful for *stretches* at a time, that I was present. I was not. I was a body in the room with a heart that had been locked away so long I had forgotten where I put the key.

Emotional unavailability is something I learned early. In my home growing up, feelings were not something you expressed. You pushed through. You handled it. You did not burden others with what was going on inside you. That programming ran deep.

* * *

The women I was with needed emotional intimacy. They needed me to be curious about their inner lives and willing to share mine. They needed conversations that went past the surface. They needed me to be moved by things, to let them see me uncertain or soft or afraid.

I could not give that. Not because I did not feel those things, but because showing them felt dangerous in a way I could not have articulated at the time. Vulnerability felt like exposure. Exposure felt like weakness. Weakness felt like an invitation for pain.

So I kept the walls up. And the women who loved me pressed their hands against those walls for years, trying to find a way in. When they finally stopped trying, I called it abandonment. I was wrong. It was exhaustion.

* * *

I remember one woman in particular asking me during an argument what I actually felt about something she had shared. Something personal, something that had taken courage for her to say. I gave her an opinion. I gave her a logical assessment. I told her what I thought about the situation in a way that was articulate and reasonable and utterly devoid of anything emotional.

She looked at me and said, I am not asking you to solve it. I am asking you to feel it with me. I did not know how to do that. I had never been taught. So I changed the subject, and she went quiet in a way that I now recognize as grief. She was grieving the version of me she had hoped might show up. She was coming to terms with the fact that he was not coming.

That memory lives in me as a kind of shorthand for everything I was getting wrong. She did not need me to fix anything. She needed me to be present. And I had spent so many years confusing action with presence that I did not even understand what she was asking for.

I understand it now. And I am learning, slowly, to give it.

4

the *truth* about dishonesty

I need to tell the truth about this, even though it is the part I am most ashamed of. I was not always faithful. Not in every relationship. There were times I sought out connection outside of where I was committed, and I told myself all the stories people tell themselves in those moments. She does not understand me. We have grown apart. This does not mean anything. All of it was false. What it meant was that I was unwilling to either fix what was broken or walk away from it honestly. So I did the cowardly thing. I stayed, and I lied.

* * *

Infidelity is not just about the physical act. It is about the ongoing deception. The looking someone in the eye and letting them believe something that is not true. The watching them love you with trust you have not earned. That is its own category of harm, and I did it, and it hurt people who deserved far better.

I also lied in smaller ways that added up. About where I had been. About what I felt. About what I wanted. I shaped the version of myself I presented carefully, showing what would keep someone close while hiding what might drive them away. That kind of dishonesty makes genuine intimacy impossible because you are never actually letting someone love the real you.

The real me was someone I was not sure was lovable. That fear drove more damage than I can fully account for. There is a cost to sustained deception that people rarely talk about, which is what it does to the person doing it. You begin to lose track of what is true. You maintain multiple versions of events, multiple faces, and over time, you become uncertain which one is actually you.

I spent years in relationships feeling deeply isolated, not because the women I was with were distant, but because I had made authentic connection impossible by lying my way into their lives. You cannot be truly known by someone you have deceived. And I craved being known. That craving and my inability to create the conditions for it to happen was one of the central contradictions of my life for a long time.

The work of becoming honest was not just about stopping the lying. It was about sitting with the discomfort of being seen without a prepared version of myself ready to go. It was about learning that the real me, with all his history and damage and contradiction, was still worth something. Still worth loving. That took a long time to believe. Some days I am still working on it.

where it aLL came from

I did not become this way on my own. That is not an excuse. But it is important context, because understanding the root of a behavior is the first step toward changing it.

I grew up in a home where love was inconsistent. Where affection could be present and warm one day and entirely withdrawn the next. Where I learned to read the emotional temperature of a room before I learned to read words on a page. Where I became an expert at managing other people's moods because my sense of safety depended on it.

That child grew into a man who replicated those patterns without realizing it. I was drawn to emotional intensity because it felt like home. I created instability in relationships because stability felt unfamiliar and, therefore, suspicious. I withheld love sometimes because love, in my earliest experience, had always come with the threat of being taken away.

* * *

None of this makes what I did acceptable. But it does make it understandable. And understanding it is what allowed me to finally interrupt it.

My therapist helped me see that I had been in a kind of emotional time loop, responding to the women in my adult life as though they were the unpredictable figures from my childhood. I was not in a relationship with them. I was in a relationship with my past, and they were paying the price for it. When that landed for me, really landed, I wept. Not for myself. For them. For every woman who had tried to love me and bumped up against wounds I had never told them about, wounds I had barely admitted to myself.

* * *

The hardest part of understanding your origins is separating explanation from excuse. I have met men who learned the same history I did and have used it as a permanent hall pass. The childhood was rough. The trauma was real. Therefore, nothing is my fault.

That is not healing. That is hiding. What my history gave me was context. What I did with that context was still my responsibility. I could have chosen to get help sooner. I could have chosen to listen when women told me what I was doing. I could have chosen to stop cycling through the same patterns once I had enough evidence that the patterns were destructive.

I did not make those choices until I was ready, and I was not ready until the cost of staying the same finally outweighed the cost of changing. That is the honest version of the story.

6

how i became this way

Nobody becomes a toxic lover on purpose. That is not an excuse. It is a fact worth sitting with, because understanding the process matters if you are ever going to interrupt it. I did not wake up one morning and decide to become someone who controlled people, withheld love, and moved through relationships, leaving damage behind. I was shaped by what I witnessed. By what was done to me. By what I was taught, explicitly and silently, about what men are, what love looks like, and what it means to need someone.

This is the chapter I was most afraid to write, because it requires me to trace the line from a child who was once innocent to a man who caused harm. That line is not comfortable to follow. But I am going to follow it anyway.

* * *

The first thing I learned about love is that it was conditional. I learned this not from a lecture but from the ordinary texture of daily life growing up. Affection arrived when I performed correctly. It withdrew when I did not. The people who were supposed to love me unconditionally, did love me, I believe that, but they expressed it in a language that came with terms attached. Be a certain way, and you will be received warmly. Step outside of that, and you will feel the cold.

A child cannot analyze this. A child simply absorbs it and builds a survival strategy around it. My strategy was to become very good at reading what was wanted from me and providing it. I learned to monitor emotional atmospheres with precision. I learned to adjust myself in real time to whatever the room required. I became, without knowing it, an expert at performance.

That skill served me in some ways. It made me perceptive, adaptable, able to navigate difficult people and situations. But it also meant that by the time I entered my first real relationship, I had almost no idea who I actually was underneath the performance. I only knew how to be what someone needed me to be. And when I could no longer figure that out, I defaulted to control.

* * *

The second thing I learned about love is that it came paired with pain. I watched the adults around me love each other in ways that were loud and volatile. Passion and punishment lived in the same house. Tenderness could flip to cruelty without warning. Someone could tell you they loved you in the morning and make you feel worthless by evening.

I internalized this as the definition of intimacy. Deep connection, I believed subconsciously, was supposed to feel like this. The intensity. The uncertainty. The way you could never quite settle because the ground kept shifting.

When I got into relationships as an adult, and they started to feel stable and calm, something in me did not trust it. Calm felt like the quiet before something bad happened. Security felt like a setup. So I would do things, sometimes consciously but more often not, that introduced turbulence. I would pick a fight that did not need to happen. I would go cold at precisely the moment things were going well. I would introduce doubt where none had existed. I was recreating what I knew. And the women who loved me suffered for it.

The third thing I learned about love is that vulnerability makes you a target. I learned this from the men around me. The message, delivered through silence and example and the occasional direct statement, was that showing your feelings was weakness. That a man who cried, who needed comfort, who admitted fear or uncertainty, was someone to be dismissed or taken advantage of.

I watched men who showed softness get punished for it, sometimes by other men, sometimes by the very women they opened up to. I filed those observations away carefully. By the time I was a teenager, I had built a wall around my interior life that I genuinely believed was protection. What it actually was, was a prison. For me and for everyone who tried to love me.

The wall kept me from being hurt in certain ways. But it also kept everything real from getting in or out. Every woman I was with was eventually pressing against that wall, trying to find the person behind it, while I stood on the other side wondering why she could not just accept things the way they were.

* * *

There is a specific moment I think about when I trace how I became this way. I was maybe twelve or thirteen years old. I had done something vulnerable, something I no longer remember exactly, but I had let someone see something real and tender in me. And the response was laughter. Not cruel laughter necessarily, but dismissive. The kind that says what you just showed me is not taken seriously.

I remember the heat of it. The way my face flushed and reconfigured, and I worked very hard to make sure no one could see that it had. I made a decision in that moment, not a conscious, thought-out decision, but a deep instinctive one, that I would not do that again. I would not give anyone that kind of access to something real in me.

I adhered to that decision for nearly thirty years. Thirty years of relationships built on a foundation of managed distance. Thirty years of women trying to reach me and finding something smooth and impenetrable where a person should have been. Thirty years of loneliness that I called independence because the alternative was admitting how afraid I was.

* * *

I also became this way through the men who modeled relationships for me. The men in my life were not villains. Most of them were doing the best they could with what they had been given. But what they had been given was a narrow and damaging definition of manhood. A man provides. A man does not ask for help. A man does not show weakness. A man takes control because the alternative is chaos.

I watched how these men move through their relationships, and I copied what I saw. I copied the detachment and called it strength. I copied the control and called it responsibility. I copied the silence and called it not being dramatic. Nobody told me that what I was copying was damage that had been passed down through generations of men who had never been given permission to be full human beings. Nobody told me that the strength I was modeling was actually armor, and that armor, worn long enough, becomes indistinguishable from the person wearing it.

* * *

At some point, the shaping stopped being something that happened to me and became something I was choosing to maintain. That is the piece that required the most honesty to accept. Because at a certain age, you have enough self-awareness to know that what you are doing is causing harm. You have been told. You have seen it. The evidence is not subtle. Yet, still I continued. I continued because change felt more dangerous than staying the same. Because the walls had been up so long that I did not know who I was without them. Because becoming a different person meant grieving the years I had spent being the wrong one, and that grief felt unbearable.

So I kept moving. Kept cycling. Kept finding new relationships and bringing the same patterns into them, and wondering why nothing ever felt right, and always ended wrong. That is how I became this way. And that is what it took to finally stop.

what i never said out LOUD

There are things I carried into every relationship that I never told anyone. I never told anyone that I was afraid every single time. That underneath the confidence, underneath the capability and the competence I projected, there was a person who was genuinely terrified of being left. Not metaphorically afraid. Functionally, physically, in-the-chest afraid. Every time I started to care about someone, the fear moved in alongside the feeling.

I never told anyone that I checked their phone, not because I thought they were doing something wrong, but because I needed constant evidence that I was still chosen. That is not jealousy. That is panic with better clothes on.

* * *

I never told anyone how much I needed to be needed. It was not about love. It was about relevance. If she needed me, she could not leave. I designed myself to be indispensable in the lives of women I was with, not out of generosity, but out of self-protection. I fixed things. I solved problems. I showed up in crisis in a way I could not show up in the ordinary moments, because I thought crisis gave me a bigger role. It gave me a reason to be there that felt earned and necessary. Ordinary presence, the kind where you just sit with someone and let the day be what it is, was much harder for me. I did not know what I could offer in those moments.

I never told anyone how lonely I was inside those relationships. That is the irony that I have had to sit with. I created connections that made it impossible to feel. I was in rooms full of people who cared about me, and I was completely alone inside my own chest.

* * *

I am telling it now because I think a lot of men are living in that same silence and calling it strength. We were taught to manage our feelings, not feel them. We were taught that the internal life is private at best and dangerous at worst. We were taught that needing things, especially emotional things, was a liability. And so we learned to take what we needed sideways, through control or distance or a hundred small manipulations that we did not have words for.

The words exist. The work exists. And the men who are willing to do it will have better lives and cause less damage. I am certain of this because I am living it.

the reckoning

At some point, understanding why you did something is not enough. You have to reckon with the fact that you did it. This chapter is that reckoning.

To the women I controlled into believing their instincts were wrong, I am sorry. You were right more often than you knew, and I worked hard to make you doubt that. You deserved someone who made you feel more certain of yourself, not less.

* * *

To the women who pressed their hands against my walls until their palms were bruised from the effort, I am sorry. Your need for emotional connection was not excessive. It was human. I was the one who was insufficient, not you.

To the women I was dishonest with, in ways large and small, I am sorry. You gave me your trust, and I treated it carelessly. There is no version of that where I was the victim. I was the one who caused harm, and you deserved the truth and the choice it would have given you.

To every woman who walked away from me feeling like she

was too much, or not enough, or somehow responsible for my inability to show up, I am sorry. You were none of those things. You were just in the wrong story with the wrong version of me.

I cannot undo any of it. What I can do is make sure the next chapter is written differently.

* * *

A real reckoning is not a public performance. I want to be clear about that. Writing this is not my absolution. I am not looking to be forgiven through honesty. The women I hurt do not owe me anything, including the grace of accepting an apology.

What a reckoning is, at its best, is a line in the ground. A moment where you look at the full scope of what you have done without flinching and then decide, from that clear-eyed place, who you are going to be from here. I have drawn that line. I intend to stay on the right side of it.

faith and the harder work

Recovery looks different from this side of the mirror. When I had been the one hurt, returning to faith felt like comfort. Like being welcomed home. When I had to return to faith as the one who had done the hurting, it felt more like standing in a courtroom and hoping for mercy. But mercy came. That is the thing about genuine faith. It does not excuse what you have done. It does not minimize the harm. But it does hold open the possibility that you are not the worst version of yourself. That you can be made new. That the work of becoming better is worth doing, even when you cannot undo what has already been done.

* * *

I began to pray differently. Not just for my own healing but for the women I had hurt. That they would find the love and peace I had failed to give them. That my absence from their lives would feel like freedom rather than loss. That God would restore what I had taken in the ways that only God can.

I also began to take seriously the spiritual call to accountability. Not performative accountability, where you confess publicly to feel better about yourself. Real accountability, which is quieter and less comfortable. It meant sitting with what I had done without immediately reaching for reassurance. It meant letting the weight of it be what it was. That weight, carried honestly, became the thing that changed me. Not guilt as punishment, but guilt as information. A signal pointing toward who I needed to become.

* * *

Faith also required me to stop using God as a shortcut. I have known men who prayed for change while refusing to do the work that prayer points toward. They wanted transformation delivered to them rather than grown through them. I had done some version of that myself. I wanted to be better in the abstract without doing the uncomfortable, concrete, unglamorous work of actually becoming better.

Therapy was part of that work. Honest conversations with people I trusted were part of that work. Reading, sitting still, learning to tolerate my own interior without running from it were all part of that work. Faith gave me the foundation and the motivation. But the work was still mine to do. Those two things together are what recovery actually looks like.

when GOD became real to me again

I want to be careful here, because faith is personal, and I am not writing this to preach at anyone. What I am writing is simply my honest account of what happened when I finally stopped running from God and started running toward Him.

For most of my adult life, I had a complicated relationship with my faith. I believed in God in the background, the way some people believe in gravity. It was there, it was real, but I did not think about it much, and I certainly did not let it change how I lived. I went through the motions when it was convenient. I prayed when I needed something. I kept God at the same arm's length; I kept everyone else. Then everything fell apart. And I ran out of arms' length.

* * *

The season that broke me open spiritually was not dramatic from the outside. There was no single catastrophic event. It was more like a slow accumulation, a weight that kept adding to itself until one day I could not carry it anymore. I had just ended another relationship badly. Not with violence or a big blowup, just with the familiar quiet wreckage I seemed to leave everywhere. She cried. I stood there, unable to give her anything real. I drove home and sat in the dark of my apartment for a long time, and for the first time, I did not try to talk myself out of how I felt.

I felt empty. Not sad exactly. Just hollow. Like I had been going through the motions of a life without actually inhabiting it. And in that hollow, quiet place, I said something out loud that I had never said before. I said, "God, I do not know how to be different. But I need to be." That was the prayer. Seven words. No eloquence. No theology. Just a man in the dark, finally admitting he was lost.

* * *

What happened next was not a lightning bolt. It was not a voice from the sky or a vision or a miraculous transformation overnight. What happened was slower and more ordinary and somehow more powerful than any of those things.

Things began to shift. I started waking up with a different quality of thought. Not positive thinking, not affirmations, but a kind of quietness that had not been there before. A sense that I was not alone with the weight of who I had been. That something larger than my own willpower was at work in the process.

I started reading scripture again, not out of obligation but out of genuine hunger. And the passages that hit me hardest were not the ones about grace and forgiveness. Though those mattered, the ones that stopped me cold were the ones about love. What it actually is. What it actually requires. First Corinthians thirteen had been read at every wedding I had ever attended, and I had heard it without ever really listening. *Love is patient. Love is kind. It does not insist on its own way. It is not irritable or resentful.* I read those words slowly this time, and I thought about every relationship I had been in, and I understood with quiet devastation how far I had been from any of it.

* * *

God did not let me off the hook. That is something I need to clearly affirm, because I think some people imagine that turning to faith means you get to skip the hard part. That you confess and repent and everything gets washed clean, and you move on unburdened. That has not been my experience. What faith gave me was not an escape from accountability. It gave me the strength to face it fully.

God held up a mirror that was clearer and more unflinching than any I had ever looked in. He showed me the pattern. He showed me the damage. He showed me the frightened child underneath all the armor who had built a whole personality around never being hurt again, and how that child had grown into a man who hurt others instead. And then, in the same breath, He showed me something else. He showed me that none of it had to be permanent. That the same God who created me had the power to remake me. Not erase what I had done, but transform who I was.

That combination, full accountability and full grace at the same time, was something I had never encountered in any human relationship. It was the first time I truly understood why people call it unconditional love. Not because God overlooked the harm, but because He refused to let the harm be the final word about who I was.

* * *

Prayer became something different for me during this time. It stopped being a wish list and became a conversation. Sometimes it was confession. I would sit quietly and just name what I had done, specifically, without softening it or reframing it. I would say it plainly and let it be what it was before God. There is something about that kind of honesty in prayer that does something to the shame. Shame thrives in silence and secrecy. When you bring something into the light, even if the only witness is God, it loses a certain kind of power over you. I stopped carrying the weight alone. I handed it over, piece by piece, and felt it become lighter in ways I cannot fully explain but know to be real.

I also started praying specifically for the women I had hurt. Not in a way that was about me or my guilt. I prayed for their healing. For the relationships that came after me to be filled with what I had failed to give. For God to meet them in the places I had left empty. Those prayers hurt at first. Over time, they became something I looked forward to. A small act of love I could offer when I had no other way to reach them.

My faith community became part of the recovery in ways I had not expected. I had always kept church at a distance, showing up enough to feel like I was honoring something without getting close enough to be accountable to anyone. When I finally let people in, genuinely in, I found something I had not had since childhood. A group of people who knew the worst of me and stayed anyway.

There were men in that community who had done their own work. Who had been where I was and had come through it. They did not judge me. They did not let me off easy either. They sat with me in the hard parts and pointed me back toward God when I started to drift. That kind of brotherhood, built on honesty and shared faith rather than performance and posturing, was entirely new to me.

I had spent my whole life keeping men at arm's length, too. Believing that real vulnerability between men was not possible or not safe. That community proved me wrong, and that proof changed me in ways that directly affected how I began to show up in every relationship.

* * *

The most important thing my faith gave me was a new identity to grow into. For so long, my identity had been built around what I could do, what I could project, and what I could control. When all of that started to fall away, I needed something to stand on. Faith gave me that foundation. It told me I was not the sum of my worst behavior. That I was made on purpose, for a purpose, and that the purpose included becoming a man who knew how to love. Not perfectly. Not without struggle. But genuinely, with my whole self, the way God intended when He designed the human heart for connection.

I am still becoming that man. I expect to be becoming him for the rest of my life. But I am no longer doing it alone, and I am no longer doing it in the dark. That, more than anything else, is what God gave back to me.

learning a new way to love

Therapy did not just help me understand my past. It taught me skills I had never developed. Things that healthy people often learn growing up, and that I had simply missed. I learned what it actually means to listen. Not to wait for my turn to speak, not to formulate my defense while the other person is still talking, but to be genuinely present with what someone is sharing and let it matter to me.

I learned to name my emotions instead of acting them out. To say I am feeling afraid right now instead of becoming controlling. To say I need some space instead of disappearing without explanation. These sound simple. They were not simple for me.

* * *

I learned what healthy boundaries look like, both setting my own and respecting someone else's. I had confused control with security for so long that the idea of a boundary as something mutual and respectful was almost foreign.

I also learned to sit with discomfort without immediately trying to fix or escape it. A lot of my toxic behavior had been a way of managing my own anxiety at someone else's expense. Learning to tolerate my own feelings without outsourcing them to the people around me was one of the most significant shifts of my adult life.

I am still learning. I expect I will be for a long time. But I know the difference now between who I was and who I am trying to become, and that distinction is real.

* * *

One of the things nobody warned me about is how strange healthy feels at first. When I started responding differently in situations that used to trigger my worst patterns, it felt unnatural. It felt like I was performing a version of myself I did not fully believe yet. My therapist told me that this was normal. That the new behavior has to be practiced before it becomes genuine. That you act your way into a new way of being before you feel your way there.

She was right. Over time, the responses that felt scripted became more natural. The space I used to fill with control or silence or deflection started to fill with something quieter and more honest. I started to be curious about people rather than strategic with them. That shift alone changed the quality of every relationship in my life.

A new way to love is not a destination. It is a daily practice, and some days I am better at it than others. But I am *in* the practice now. That is what matters.

the MAN i AM choosing to become

I do not get to call myself healed. I do not think that is how it works. What I can say is that I am awake now in a way I was not before. I see my patterns. I feel them rising before I act on them. I have people in my life, a therapist, trusted friends, a faith community who know the truth about who I have been and are invested in who I am becoming. That kind of accountability is not comfortable. It is necessary.

I am learning to be in relationships differently. To show up with my actual self rather than a curated performance. To ask questions with an actual desire to know the answer. To let someone's feelings land without immediately making them about me. To be honest, even when honesty is inconvenient.

* * *

I have not been in a serious relationship since I began this work. Not because I have given up on love, but because I understand now that I need to be a certain kind of person before I can be a healthy partner. I am not there yet. But I am closer than I have ever been.

If you are reading this and you recognize yourself in the person I was, I want you to know that recognition is not condemnation. It is an invitation. The fact that you can see it means you are already further along than you think. You caused harm. So did I. That is true, and it has to be held. But it does not have to be the end of the story. The story can change. You can change. Not perfectly, not all at once, but genuinely and over time, in ways that matter. That is what I am betting my life on.

* * *

Becoming is not a single event. It is a direction. Some days, the direction is clear, and the walking is steady. Other days, I stray from the path and have to find it again. Both are part of the process, and I have stopped expecting it to be otherwise. What I am choosing, actively and repeatedly, is to keep going. To not let the weight of who I was become an excuse to stay that person. To take seriously the possibility that the man I am becoming is someone worth being, and that the relationships ahead of me can be built on something real. That choice, made fresh every morning, is the work. It is the only work that matters.

epilogue

To the man reading this who knows, somewhere underneath all the justifications, that he has been the problem Welcome. It took courage to get here.

The road from recognizing the harm to actually changing is long, and it is not linear. There will be days you slip back into old patterns and have to begin again. There will be moments of clarity so sharp they hurt. There will be grief for the relationships you damaged and the person you could have been sooner. Let all of it be part of the process. None of it disqualifies you from becoming someone better.

Find a therapist. Lean into your faith. Tell the truth to someone who can handle it. Build a life where honesty is the foundation rather than the exception. And when you are ready to love again, love differently. Love with everything you have learned about yourself, including the hard parts.

The women in your past deserved better. The woman in your future deserves the man you are becoming.

Do the work. All of it. It is worth it.

— James D. Ferguson

reflection

What Toxic Love Looks Like

Use this space to write down what toxic love has looked like in your own life. Be honest. No one else has to read this.

reflection

What Healthy Love Looks Like

Now write down what healthy love looks like to you. What does it feel like? What does it require of you? What kind of partner do you want to become?

James D. Ferguson was born in Benton Harbor, Michigan, and now resides in Columbus, Ohio. Raised in an urban environment, he faced and overcame significant challenges that shaped his drive and determination to reach his dreams. Through the guidance of mentors and the influence of his grandfather, William A. Ferguson, James transformed his life, becoming a successful business owner, real estate investor, and entrepreneur.

As the founder of the Self Made Brand, James operates a jewelry business, clothing line, and fragrance line, building a legacy rooted in growth, accountability, and purpose. Alongside his professional success, James is candid about his personal challenges, including his struggles with relationships and unhealthy patterns involving women. Rather than hide from those experiences, he has chosen to confront them, using self-reflection, faith, and fellowship to grow into a more self-aware, disciplined, and emotionally responsible human being.

A devoted father of five and proud grandfather, James is deeply committed to becoming better in every area of his life and helping others do the same. Through his expanding book series, he shares both his successes and his shortcomings, offering transparent lessons on mentorship, networking, relationships, and personal accountability. His work reflects a powerful truth: real growth begins with honesty, and lasting change is possible through faith, community, and the willingness to do the work.

COMING SOON!

"Green-Eyed Loved Ones"

Green-Eyed Loved Ones is a powerful look at how jealousy can quietly exist within the closest relationships. This book uncovers the subtle ways envy shows up, often masked as concern, and how it can strain even the closest bonds. Through reflection and real-life insight, James encourages readers to recognize these patterns, set healthy boundaries, and protect their peace. Sometimes your loved ones despise your shine.

"Just a Kid from Benton Harbor"

Just a Kid from Benton Harbor is more than a story about where James is from; this book breaks down how environment, choices, and mindset collide to shape a life. James shares the realities of navigating ambition and identity while trying to build something long-lasting. It's not a polished success story, but an honest look at growth, pressure, and figuring things out in real time, from survival to Self-Made.

The Entrepreneurial Success Series is AVAILABLE NOW WHERE BOOKS ARE SOLD

"The Power of Networking" marks the inaugural volume in James D. Ferguson's series. Within the pages of this insightful work, Ferguson shares his personal journey, shedding light on the crucial role networking played in shaping his path to success. As he delves into the lessons learned and the doors opened through meaningful connections, the narrative provides practical advice on effectively leveraging networking to propel one's career forward. With a wealth of experience as a thriving entrepreneur in diverse industries such as real estate, jewelry, and fashion, James stands as a living testament to the transformative power of strategic networking. His story illuminates the intricate path for young black men and other individuals navigating the complexities of the business world, offering a tangible road to winning in business through the cultivation of meaningful professional relationships.

"The Power of Mentorship" is a call to action where readers will find inspiration, guidance, and a renewed belief in their potential to succeed. In the pages of this compelling work, James D. Ferguson opens up about the pivotal role mentors played in shaping his trajectory. He explores the lessons learned, the wisdom gained, and the doors opened by those who believed in him. The book serves as a roadmap for aspiring entrepreneurs, providing practical advice on building a successful career and business. Ferguson's story is not only a source of motivation but a blueprint for leveraging mentorship to overcome challenges and create opportunities, particularly for young Black men seeking to navigate the complexities of the business world. James' success in the real estate, jewelry, and fashion industry is a living testament to the transformative power of mentorship.

COMING SOON!

"The Power of Perception"
"The Power of Leadership"
"The Power Within You"

Go to www.selfmadelimitedco.com and www.flexyogrill.com to learn more about James D. Ferguson's books and business success.

www.ingramcontent.com/pod-product-compliance
Lightning Source LLC
LaVergne TN
LVHW020313110826
845148LV00017BA/2645

* 9 7 9 8 9 8 6 6 9 4 1 3 9 *